The Kenmare Occurrences

The Kenmare Occurrences

Poems by

Harry White

Kelsay Books

© 2018 Harry White. All rights reserved. This material may not be reproduced in any form, published, reprinted, recorded, performed, broadcast, rewritten or redistributed without the explicit permission of Harry White. All such actions are strictly prohibited by law.

Cover: Muckross Abbey, Killarney, Co. Kerry

ISBN: 978-1-947465-72-5

Kelsay Books
Aldrich Press
www.kelsaybooks.com

Acknowledgements

My best thanks to Marc Caball, Ron Callan, Brian Donnelly, Peter Donnelly, Porscha Fermanis, Margaret Kelleher, Declan Kiberd and Linda Morra for having read and commented upon some of these poems. I am especially grateful to Chantel Lavoie, whose incisive criticism and technical advice are matched only by her humane encouragement as a fellow practitioner.

I would also like to express my gratitude to Karen Kelsay and Sarah Stark for their editorial care in the production of this book.

Contents

New Year's Eve	9
Lights	10
Slides	11
Old Photographs	13
Living Quarters	14
French Windows	15
The Spare Room	16
Martley Drive	17
A Softness	18
The Kenmare Occurrences	19
Court Music, 1730	21
Among School Children	22
The Dressmaker	23
A Border Crossing	27
Arrivals	28
The Pier	29
National Airs	30
A Translation	31
Inscriptions	32
Place Names	33
The Portly Communions of Middle Age	34
Time Signatures	35
A Fossil from Georgian Bay	36
The First Time	37

About the Author

New Year's Eve

> *'How you hugged me, how you danced with joy!'* she exclaimed ten years later, in the course of inventing a brand-new past.
> —Nabokov, *Speak, Memory*

The black-billed mouthpiece cradled in her palm,
Her fingers closed around its gleaming hood,
She's laughing into the phone on New Year's Eve.

The whole tableau is American, from the movies:
Her signature cocktail dress in black, her brooch,
Her unattended cigarette,
The haze and glow of street lights,
Softened in the pane of glass behind her.

There is no trace of Dublin, Greentrees Road.

It's over in a moment,
This other life,
Imagined in the shutter-swift exposure
Of that sleek, expensive Kodak
He's aiming at her now.

She winces at the flash, gives up the phone,
Yields to the tumult of relatives in the hall,
The tides and slow immersions
Of her motherhood.

The photo, meanwhile, outlasts fifty years.
Its birdlike grace still holds and saddens me,
As well as the scrawl in sloppy biro
Across its glossy margin:
Sheila calling Canada, '63

Lights

When the film was threaded and ready to run,
Someone would shout 'Lights!'
The darkened room a silhouette of bobbing heads
Against the splash and flood of colour on the wall or screen.
Impromptu cries of recognition, laughter ('I can't see!')
Would punctuate the steady, metrical whirr,
The rivulet of feeding tape
We knew would last three minutes and no more.

This hand-held life.

Then awkward panoramas kept our gaze:
The downward, shy refusals in the glare of sun
Of startled aunts, or straight-to-camera children
In the sand, quizzical, smiling, glad to show their wares,
Or solitary, heedless of the family fuss:
A little girl intent upon her dolls
Underneath the baby grand piano.
An infant frowning at a bracelet.

Our inadvertent neighbour primly waves
Unsteady greetings, as the camera sweeps
Across the afternoon
And gutters into darkness.

The lights are switched back on.
Relatives, now long dead, resume
The everyday scenario of their lives:
They grope for car-keys, cigarettes,
Or mime departure to their patient wives.
Everyone blinks in the sudden surge of light.
A silent camera follows them into the night.

Slides

Grandma Ross is sulking at her son:
'Edmund, put those slides away!
I hate those silly pictures in the dark'.
Her baleful glance, her clownish, downturned mouth,
A trout expiring on a slab of ice,
Or so she seemed to me when I was nine.

But Edmund ('Eamon' to his wife and friends)
Does not repine, or lessen his enchantment.
He loads the carousel with squinted slides,
And preps its dull exposures.

Ejection and re-load:
I like the double-slotted sound,
The swift report
Which heralds each new slide,
The old one, like a cartridge, spent and gone.

The carousel, alas, goes on and on,
Projecting Uncle Eamon's bland retrievals
Of family life:
'The seaside at Kenmare'; 'Two donkeys kissing';
A guesthouse called 'El Carmen'.
It is as if each fresh, descending frame
Annuls the hope its imminence portended,
And then confirms the dreariness of the whole.

The slides in Grandma Ross's head (and mine)
Are very different.
She'll never share them with her obtuse son:
'The fat priest in Ballinasloe with fingers';
'The orphanage in Clare Street';

'Baby John'.
She shuts her blank fish-eyes against the glare
Of Eamon's boy-scout, campsite-glee projections
And dozes off into the dark somewhere
His camera cannot reach.

He, meanwhile, continues.
'Ladies' View'; 'Our fishing trip in Wexford':
An eager close-up of the bloodied catch,
Dead, or barely breathing, on the beach.

Old Photographs

He is all tolerant smiles and easy demeanour,
Handsome, seated front-square in the frame.
She is leaning right across his shoulder,
Careless and jubilant, laughing, stroking his arm.

His grin is tightening into a veiled endurance:
'Let this end soon', he thinks, 'this lovers' pose.'
She is unguarded and far too relaxed to notice
The signatures of withdrawal in his face.

Photographs acquire an ultimate meaning
As the years confirm what happened next:
I was the girl, and *you* were the boy contriving
To slip away. Now I feel less perplexed.

Living Quarters

This was new when I was born:
The blank estate of houses built on farms,
'Road', 'Park', 'Avenue', 'Close' or 'Gardens',
Red-roofed subdivisions tightly spaced
Around the fading villages they adjoined.

We loved the older places best—'The shops',
The laneway leading to forbidden fields
That lay beyond our firm encampment:
Something beautiful and unsafe.

The others ran to meet it.
I held back,
But nursed its rival promises all the more
Within the servile concrete and the tree-lines
That bordered my enchantment with obedience.

In middle age the others have returned
To live within the maze again,
While I prepare to leave.
However uncertain this journey, however late,
Their haven is for me a ghost estate.

French Windows

In six weeks the walls came down
And new foundations were filled up
With concrete.
I saw the mix going in,
So full and thick and milky soft,
But next day, hard and sullen.

The word itself filled up like that:
'We're building an *extension*'—
That lovely middle stress,
Its elongated, leisurely caress
A gloss upon some harmless portent.

After a while,
The word rose in my gorge
As if I were trying to swallow it.
'Extension' meant erasure:
The trim composure of the house was gone,
The walls torn down,
The secret meaning of the older rooms
Annulled,
The long back garden halved.

So when at last we tumbled in upon
The bright new rooms,
Engorging all that lustrous, gleaming space,
I felt the plaintive phantom of French windows
That gave onto the garden weeks before
And framed the small enchantment of that place,
Now swallowed up by the hard, laminate floor.

The Spare Room

The Spare Room was the stranger's room.
It lodged the spinster aunt or irksome nun,
Or one of our beautiful cousins on the run
From awful Uncle Tommy and Stepmother Joan.

Everything there was for someone who lived alone:
A single bed, an upright chair, a chest of drawers,
A print of the Child of Prague, a vase of flowers,
A view of the toy-strewn garden after hours.

When heavenly Susan came with auburn hair
And passed the night in tears in my mother's arms
She slept in that room, and went to London from there.
It held her warmth. The rest is her affair.

Martley Drive

For Jose Matera

I love the morning sounds this house affords:
The stove-hiss of coffee, the percolation
Of radio, bedroom cadences,
Birdsong. Wakening words.

The low, warm burble of American,
And sunlight streaming through the hall
Soften the taunts and silences
Of last night's withdrawal.

Ghost-faced and grey, the laptop screen in my room
Readies itself for more of the same:
The iron rod of reproof,
Or some fresh dalliance. Or blame.

A humming bird, tremulous, visitant, on the deck
Distracts me from all this when I step out
To inhale the Canadian air.
Then it's no longer there.

A Softness

Mr Morrison makes the nurses quiver
While barren, would-be mothers in his wake
Implore his science, scrape the fees together
For his scrapings.
Futile, *cowed*, they take
His waiting rooms, his 'chorus lines',
Whatever quips his scalpel wit affords.

He wants results.

His nasal, Bristol whine
Beneath the surgical-robber mask
Is foreign here, and suited to bad news:
'Even gynaecologists get the blues.
The nurse will show you out.'

Dazed, contrite and angry,
Watch that woman leave
As Morrison does his professorial best
To cultivate a softness on the airwaves:
His 'radio voice', his lullaby compassion
Would move a Petri dish to tears.

Back on the ward,
The plundering clinician reappears,
Assyrian in his judgements, brisk and clever,
As tightening couples bless his name for ever.

The Kenmare Occurrences

My Dublin betters summoned me for this:
A magic-lantern show, an Irish 'Lourdes'.
For this, my Roman tailor said goodbye,
And I was sent from all that I held dear.
Obedient, exiled, kissed and on my way,
'Appointed to Kenmare'.
They told me I was needed there
To regulate the faithful in their frenzy,
The Marian hysteria of those girls.

'Tell his Lordship what you saw',
They sent me back for this!
'I seen the Virgin Mary fourteen times',
This tribal, voodoo *nonsense*.
                    What is worse,
Those oafish men colluded with the peasants:
Medieval friars intent on shrines
And relics, splinters of the holy cross.
Shambolic, servile, stiff-necked, balding priests,
Temperance-mongering fantasists.
I must contain myself.

I longed for Rome, the sunny, marble refuge
From all this, the avenues and incense-laden glory
I'd loved and almost owned, until that cardinal
Had Judas-kissed my cheek and sent me back
As bishop to this ancient, stagnant place,
This pagan, rural wilderness and kingdom
Of the dull and superstitious.

That day, that very day when I set forth
In 1964 from Rome

To take possession of my dismal See,
The nuns were grooming children for my reverence,
And 'fairest flowers'—those Marian apparitions—
Began to bloom.

I could not cut them down.
I could not irrigate the sludge and sand
Of those dark minds with Roman springs.
And who was I to stem the supernatural?
The Virgin sighted in the windy fields,
Or plaster statues said to move at night:
How could I vouch for these occurrences
Or even understand them, try as I might?

Court Music, 1730

For Lorenz Welker

Must *everything* be sung?—all sentiments
Raised up on stilts of sound in arch Italian,
My grammatical harpsichord governing this and that
Extravagance of love? The 'storm-tossed seas',
The turbulence of the well-to-do
In gilt salons: this has been my lot
For almost forty years. I nurse them through
Their 'rages' and their 'thought-tormented' tears.

It's much the same in church. I supervise
Imperial supplications sent on high,
His corpulent Majesty dozing through the incense
And dreaming of the hunt:
Exhausted stags and trumpeters,
The slump of wounded flesh,
A mad percussion of horses' hooves and gunshot
And furtive refuge in the servants' tent.

I sometimes wish I were away from this,
In Hirtenfeld: no music, just a winter's evening sky
Showing the northern star and a crescent moon
In wide, pale bands of blue.
No machines, vestments or paint
And no preposterous opera, running late.
I pine for wet fields and silence in the long grass.
The blaze of an innkeeper's grate. A warmed glass.

Among School Children

Tranquil dusk on Merton Road.
His shadow fell across the careful verges,
The hedgerows trim and spruce,
Those English laneways he had come to love,
The Queen Anne grace and refuge of the houses
That blessed his nimble progress down the street.

They liked his Scottish burr around those parts,
The Glasgow salt and shrewdness
Which gleamed like a half-hidden blade whenever he spoke.
They liked his sermons too:
'Humane and clever.
He preached so *awfully* well. He was very discrete'.

So when the writs were issued and words like 'rape'
And 'children' and 'grievous assault' were used,
These blameless, pastoral, English afternoons
Were ruptured and defaced. Thus accused,
He answered the allegations with his life,
An act of contrition made from mortal grief.

Or was it rather from shame? And who could know?
I can picture him yet with merry, coal-dark eyes
And quizzical mouth: the *kindness* of the man!
I cannot imagine the demon they had drawn.
Exposed, disgraced, or even by some forgiven,
How could one tell the sinner from such a sin?

The Dressmaker

Weak tea in the slants of afternoon,
The slope of Larkfield Gardens
From the sewing-room upstairs,
Where Margaret works in 1989:

The hemline of a wedding dress
Or christening robe
And punctuated silences
-A motorized tattoo-
Tell you that she's there,
But not much more.

Her hands are getting sore.

A thousand soft depressions of her foot
To regulate the needlework,
Like mild accelerations, pace the hours.
Or mother, whistling, staring into space,
And tapping her foot to mindless time downstairs.

This has gone on for years:

Her prayers and firm novenas,
Her Joyful Mysteries on Mount Argus Road,
Her motorbike excursions to the sea,
A laughing passenger waving it all away –
The pain, the spinster-solitudes,
And something that she mentions every day.

Margaret isn't shy, or beaten down,
A Gretchen chained and pining at her wheel,
A tragic seamstress at the sewing-machine.

She's nearer in the flame to God
And trusts His mad diversions.

At seventy-one, and just below her knee
The sorrowful, wooden mystery
That maimed her life in 1928
When she was ten.

'The accident', she calls it,
And 'the woodener', her prosthesis.
These are bearable shorthands for the wound,
Which must be expiated and atoned
Each time she's swamped in decent, human warmth,
The nieces she adores,
And all of family life she might have owned.

Instead,
A blind acceleration of events
Destroys all this in seconds:
She's on the snowy pavement with her sister,
Emerging from the church. Their arms are linked,
With Grandma just behind.
A black car lurches, mounts the icy footpath
And lunges for the kill: two out of three,
Her left leg smashed against the churchyard wall.

God, in His mercy, blanks out all the rest:
The bodies tossed and lifeless on the street
As people scream and stare,
The blood-red snow, the ripped-up seams of flesh

And severed limbs of children,
The wanton stupefaction of His presence.

Unconscious, unaware,
Only she and He survive.

A marriage made in heaven, you could say:
God, in His sparrow-falling, inexplicable way,
Tending to her stitches, sutures, fittings,
The orthopaedic terrors of her childhood,
While she converts all this to His good grace,
Demented by His kindness.

Then a space of sixty years in which
He leaves her to herself, her own devices:
Stitches, fittings, dresses, christening robes,
Her fingers nursing the cloth beneath the needle,
Her right foot on the pedal, gently applied,
So that nothing is torn or shredded.

This much is deeply embedded:
Her garments are made for girls, or brides-to-be,
Who love their shapely, attentive, bodily grace.
She nods and smiles with pleasure at work well done,
She fingers each riveted hem and crease,
Admires the giddy sway of her radiant niece
Emerging, free of the church, into the sun,
Wearing the white perfection of her gown.
But through those six mysterious decades
Of uncomplaining pain,
Not once has she sewn a stitch for boys
Or for men.

Weak tea in the slants of afternoon.
God is coming soon.

She makes her way along Mount Argus Road
And sways into the street.
Distracted by the mid-novena trance
She's in, by prayers and musings, going it alone,
She's knocked clean off her feet
And falls like a mannequin under the screeching car.

The ways of God are far too far.
No-one, not even she,
Could stay His infernal appetite for three,
Or comprehend
The pitiless symmetry
Of that death.

And nor can I.

Walk free from the cant of afterlife,
From God's prosthetic will,
From the hospital ward in 1991,
Your work is done.

Stay inscribed in the kindnesses which you wrought,
Like a seamstress making sense of the shapeless cloth.

A Border Crossing

When the train stopped dead in no-man's land
The silence was immediate and strange:
Voices floated down the awkward carriages,
Abnormally loud in the loss of sound and range.
A power-cut stillness stranded the afternoon;
Passengers, restive and craning, or slumped and mute,
Felt its enveloping pressure: 'We'll be on our way soon',
'Does anyone know where we are?' 'We just have to wait'.

Then tall and sudden, the guards were on, advancing
Down the train, with cries of 'passport!, control!'
They were holster-hipped, impassive. Some were glancing
At faces and documents: surrender, appraisal, return.
A general surge of relief, an exhalation
Collected itself when they'd gone and the engine re-started,
Restoring the current of sound and life-giving motion
Which everyone felt the moment we departed.

Arrivals

—After *Cargoes*, by John Masefield

Crisis on the tarmac with sirens wailing,
A turbo-prop, commuter plane shudders as it lands,
With twenty-four air-sick, white-faced passengers
Stumbling down the gangway, or holding hands.

Taxi drivers standing with hand-held name cards,
Staring at the frosted doors which part, then close
On eager face-scans, trolley-surges, hastenings,
Or the solitude of travellers whom no-one knows.

Business class from Kennedy and graceful touchdown,
The affluent Atlantic, then the rich, green coast:
While a girl aboard the easeful plane is flirting on her cell phone,
Her lover in Arrivals waits an hour at most.

The Pier

For Lorraine Byrne Bodley

The pier looks out to sea
Against the dark expanse,
A pulse of implacable triplets
Washing over the obdurate stone.

It stretches like a present tense
That promenades the future:
The ungovernable swell and tide
Of things to come.

In finer weather,
Couples, strolling there,
Kiss, then stare.
Their fingers lock and tighten in the gaze.

They've come to where it ends,
To something like a point of no return:
The wide, warm avenue of the pier,
And then the waves.

Only they can know what's really there:
The secret intimacy of sea and stone
Affirming their radiant vows,
Or sending them home.

National Airs

For Una Hunt

Father thought the company 'very fine':
Lord Moira, Fitzroy (sporting epaulettes)
Fresh from his regiment. A countess in shot silk
And ostrich plumes near the piano. The Earl of Moyne.
Kilkenny marble, a window-sash, the blazing grate,
Corsets, uniforms, warm pools of light,
Liveried servants with decanted wine,
Clabby and Derwent at cards. London rain.

The ladies motioned for silence as Moore began,
A harmony 'just sufficient to bear the voice'
Beneath his 'nearly spoken' Irish songs:
'The ranks of death'. Attachments. Ancient loss.
'Such things are best left fugitive, unreclaimed.
Ireland needs good government', Derwent said.
Sarah, Lady Seton, gravely agreed
(Her work on 'agrarian virtue' vastly admired).

All in this remembrance are now dead –
Moore, the Countess, Fitzroy (hanged by the French),
And Father, dreaming of Sloperton near the end,
Whispering national airs. He'd felt the wrench
Of exile not in London, but at home:
A warden of wasted estates not his own.
Walking the blighted fields, he longed for her,
Lodged in that Georgian enchantment years before.

A Translation

Und was du suchst liegt immer hinter dir
　　　　　—Goethe, *Proserpina*

I felt the sandy grass beneath my feet,
Her almost-amorous fingers on my back,
Her breath upon my face. The summer heat
Had loosened us. Too late I knew the wrack
Of imminent departure and desire—
Her grave goodbyes, assurances of love,
Would soon be out of reach, would soon expire
Beneath the freight of family life. Above
The blue-on-blue horizon of that day
The memory of her loveliness still hovers,
The massive train which carried her away
Hurtles through the decades, parting lovers.
In its wake, the truth, though I might find you:
And what you seek forever lies behind you.

Inscriptions

In one of those twelve-hour silences often endured
In Dublin, Longford, London, the Cromwell Road,
He idles over a barrow of second-hand books
And scans abandoned titles:
*The Rings of Saturn, The Songs of Thomas Moore,
Early English Martyrs, Americans at War....*

Someone's history has been tossed in there,
Lost among the foxed and faded boards,
—The lettering on the spines like blurred inscriptions
On old, unvisited gravestones—
Or hidden in the meaningless inventory
Of soft covers whitening in the sun.

He pulls one volume from the barrow's hoard,
Reads aloud what's written on the flyleaf,
And carefully restoring it, walks away.
Here's what it has to say:
I love you so much. It will be okay with us.
Words worn down by the truth. Also a kiss.

Place Names

For Valerie Elliott

I Albany Avenue

Albany, Jane, Finch, the long vowel of *Bloor*,
College & Ossington, Yonge, Queen's Park, the Lakeshore:
This stranger's litany of place names, deep in snow
Or midsummer heat, this summons is mine by heart.
Like the lurch and halt of streetcars that stop and start
From chanted intersections, I am borne
Along the grid of memory by these sounds:
The wide, extravagant cadence of *Spadina*
The refuge and solace preserved in King & Cowan
Undimmed by the absence and elsewhere of thirty years.
Something for me of the garrison town abides
In *Dundas, Simcoe, Dupont*: like empty trains
When spoken aloud, asleep in an endless siding.
But the haven of Albany Avenue—this remains.

II Donnybrook Green

I thought of stately iambics and dactyls unspoilt,
An imagined ode to Dublin before the Great War:
Sackville, Heytesbury, Westmoreland, Merrion Square,
St James's Gate, the Rotunda, Sandymount Strand.
But the inborn subversion of Irish has weakened this end
And unsettled the solemn recital and pomp of empire.
So I want to loosen my tongue and splash out the wine
And toast instead the surrender of 'Donnybrook Green',
And the formal constraints of this sonnet to Valerie Cowan.
Let her disarm this poem as she enters a room,
And softly commands and completes it. Let her dissolve
Its procession of place names. Let her appear. And soon.
No finer avowal of poetry than her embrace,
The relief of her beauty and love. Her sense of place.

The Portly Communions of Middle Age

The portly communions of middle age
are often male and white:
Ernst in his basement, with Prussian scars
and drinking vows 'from tits to groin'
among his after-dinner men.
The women stay upstairs.

His den is like the forest floor,
but snug beneath the frost-line.
A stretch of carpet, motionless friends,
wilderness stories, campsite yarns:
grazing moose in a midnight lake.
A nightcap. Someone yawns.

Later, drowsing between the sheets
after his stiff ascent to bed,
Ernst thinks of the silent room:
A still life of cigarettes
and half-empty bottles, that winter night…
Then he turns out the light.

Time Signatures

A revelation set among my stars
                                   —Seamus Heaney, *Station Island*

In 1974,
the boy in school beside him writes
eyes of China blue
and copies the rest of the song by heart.

In 1994,
Uma Thurman chants a name
—an easeful, downward trochee—
in cooed, seductive, sing-song thirds.

Another twenty years go by:
the woman he thought had come to stay
mistakes this name for his,
corrects herself, but does not stay.

In 1974,
the boy in school beside him writes
no hope was left in sight.
He can't understand this. Later, he might.

A Fossil from Georgian Bay

For Kent Gillespie

He coaxed it with soft hammer-blows
From the lakeshore drift of shale:
A slate-grey, triangular wedge of rock
Gleaming with wetness in the afternoon.
He'd fetched it from the lake with craftsman's hands
But these are my imagined hands,
Reaching into the tidal wash of words
To gloss the dark compaction of the shale
And trace its fossil imprint.

Its weight and shape are wondrously set off
By the graven creature pressed upon the surface
Whose fan-tailed, dorsal spray and supple spine
Are smoothly embossed and formed in perfect ridges
Like a hallmark, or an assay on the stone.

Without this stamp, this age-attested image,
Impressed three hundred million years ago
On an otherwise blank slate,
This wedge of shale on my desk for sixteen years
 Is a commonplace paperweight.
But the fossil quickens the stone, deposits meaning,
And leaves a braille-feel in its wake,
Beyond its own deep signatures of life.
This is what I meant to follow here:
Anterior to its exoskeletal trace
And sensual intelligence the stone admits
Some natural kinship between me and it.

To press this might entail a ruinous mistake,
As if his hammer had slipped that day on the lake.

The First Time

Irish singers often find their pitch
By having a go at the opening phrase:
The first time...
A gravelly start, half-spoken, after which
The voice ascends and orbits round the tune,
Getting into range:
The first time I saw her...
A fractional pause and then the plunge,
Like a boat against the harbour wall
That pushes out to sea:
*The first time I saw her
Was in the month of May...*

Emboldened, under sail, the song climbs clear,
Becomes its own trajectory, billows out
Upon its voyage from then to now
Along the rise and fall and wave of melody.

Back on shore, the singer quits the song
By speaking the last few words: a gruff goodbye
To art and all that shapely enterprise
Of lungs, words and air.
Something relapses or vanishes—I'm not sure—
But *The first time I saw her* is always there.

About the Author

Harry White was born in Dublin in 1958. He was educated in Dublin and Toronto, where he was awarded the University of Toronto's E.J. Pratt medal for poetry in 1984. He is Professor of Music at University College Dublin and well known for his work as a musicologist and cultural historian. Among his academic publications are *Music and the Irish Literary Imagination* (Oxford, 2008) and *The Encyclopaedia of Music in Ireland* (Dublin, 2013), which he edited with Barra Boydell. He published his first collection of poems, *Polite Forms*, with Carysfort Press (Dublin) in 2012.

www.ingramcontent.com/pod-product-compliance
Lightning Source LLC
LaVergne TN
LVHW021627080426
835510LV00019B/2783